Baby Mine

A Mother's Love Knows No Bounds

PHOTOGRAPHY BY
TRACY RAVER & KELLEY RYDEN

SELLERS
PUBLISHING

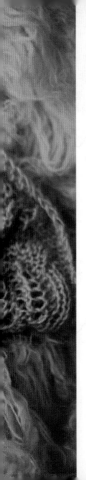

Sometimes the smallest
things take up the most room
in your heaRt.

A. A. MILNE

We came into the WORLD
like brother and brother; and
now let's go hand in hand,
not one before the other.

WILLIAM SHAKESPEARE

Sometimes when you pick up
your child you can feel the map
of your own bones beneath your
hands, or smell the scent of your
skin in the nape of his neck.
This is the most extraordinary
thing about motherhood —
finding a piece of yourself
separate and apart that all the
same you could not live without.

JODI PICOULT

If I have a monument
in this world,
it is my son.

MAYA ANGELOU

It is the nature of babies

to be in bliss.

DEEPAK CHOPRA

The children we bring into the world are small replicas of ourselves and our husbands; the pride and joy of grandfathers and grandmothers. We dream of being mothers, and for most of us those dreams are realized naturally. For this is . . . the miracle of life.

AZELENE WILLIAMS

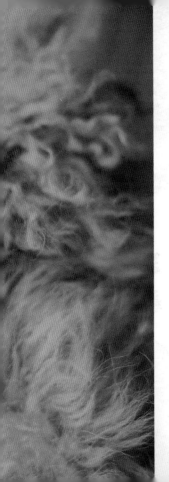

Giving birth and
being born brings us into
the essence of creation,
where the human spirit
is courageous and
bold and the body,
a miracle of wisdom.

HARRIETTE HARTIGAN

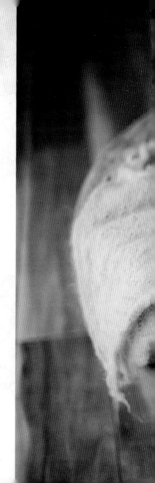

You were born together, and together you shall be forevermore. . . . But let there be spaces in your togetherness, and let the winds of the heavens dance between you.

KAHLIL GIBRAN

Sweet baby of mine,
you embraced my heart
and stole my breath away.

AUTHOR UNKNOWN

There's really nothing

quite so sweet as

tiny little baby feet.

AUTHOR UNKNOWN

I'll love you forever,
I'll like you for always.
As long as I'm living,
my baby you'll be.

ROBERT MUNSCH

Children Reinvent
your world for you.

AUTHOR UNKNOWN

In the sheltered simplicity
of the first days after a baby
is born, one sees again the
magical closed circle,
the miraculous sense
of two people existing
only for each other.

ANNE MORROW LINDBERGH

I think, at a child's birth,
if a mother could ask a fairy
godmother to endow it with
the most useful gift, that
gift should be curiosity.

ELEANOR ROOSEVELT

Every child begins
the world again. . . .

HENRY DAVID THOREAU

Love is the greatest gift
that one generation
can leave to another.

RICHARD GARNETT

Giving birth is a transformation, and it doesn't matter whether you've had eight babies before. It's still a transformation the next time you have another baby, because you are no longer the same woman you were before you had that baby.

PENNY HANDFORD

Hearts entwined,

twenty fingers,

twenty toes,

two sweet babies

with cheeks of rose.

Born on the same day,

two gifts from above,

lives entwined,

two babies to love.

AUTHOR UNKNOWN

(how to calm a crying baby) You lay your hand against his skin and just Rub his back. Blow into his ear. Press that baby up against your own skin and walk outside with him, where the night air will surround him, and moonlight fall on his face. Whistle, maybe. Dance. Hum. Pray.

JOYCE MAYNARD

A new baby is
like the beginning
of all things —
wonder, hope,
a dream of
possibilities.

EDA J. LESHAN

Birth is an opportunity to transcend. To rise above what we are accustomed to, to reach deeper inside ourselves than we are familiar with, and to see not only what we are truly made of, but the strength we can access in and through birth.

MARCIE MACARI

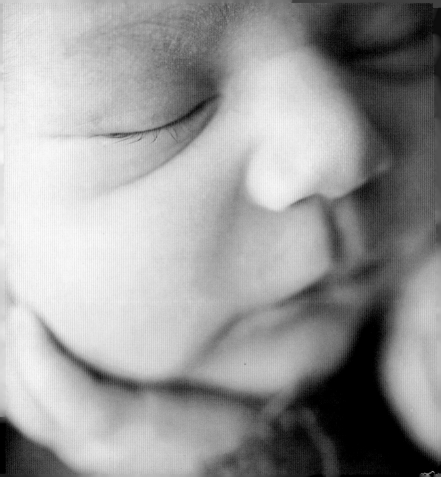

There was a never a child so lovely, but his mother was glad to get him to sleep.

RALPH WALDO EMERSON

Birth is the sudden
opening of a window,
through which you look out
upon a stupendous prospect.
For what has happened?
A miracle. You have
exchanged nothing for the
possibility of everything.

WILLIE DIXON

A baby will make
love stronger, days shorter,
nights longer, bankroll
smaller, home happier,
clothes shabbier, the past
forgotten, and the future
worth living for.

AUTHOR UNKNOWN

It was the tiniest thing I ever decided
to put my whole life into.

TERRI GUILLEMETS

A first child is your own best foot
forward, and how you do cheer those
little feet as they strike out. You examine
every turn of flesh for precocity, and
crow it to the world. But the last one: the
baby who trails her scent like a flag of
surrender through your life when there
will be no more coming after — oh,
that's love by a different name.

BARBARA KINGSOLVER

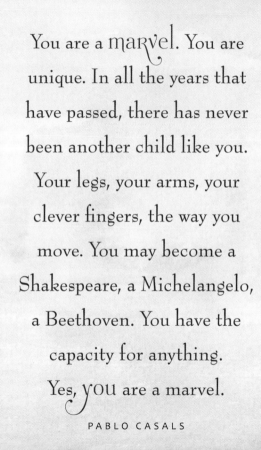

You are a marvel. You are unique. In all the years that have passed, there has never been another child like you. Your legs, your arms, your clever fingers, the way you move. You may become a Shakespeare, a Michelangelo, a Beethoven. You have the capacity for anything. Yes, you are a marvel.

PABLO CASALS

Before you were conceived,
I wanted you. Before you were born,
I loved you. Before you were here an hour,
I would give my life for you.
This is the miracle of life.

MAUREEN HAWKINS

Newborns reminded her
of tiny buddhas.

JODI PICOULT

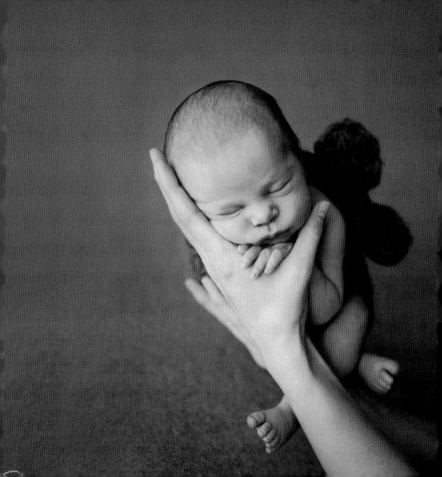

Your children will become
what you are; so be what
you want them to be.

DAVID BLY